тake тнaт:
Our Story

Piers Morgan

B🌿XTREE

First published in Great Britain in 1993 by Boxtree Limited

Text © Piers Morgan 1993.
Photographs supplied by Take That. All tour photographs © Dave Hogan 1993.
The right of Piers Morgan to be identified as Author of this Work has been asserted by him in accordance with the Copyright, Designs and Patents Act 1988.
10 9 8 7 6 5 4 3 2 1

Designed and typeset by ArtAtac Design
Printed and bound in Great Britain by Cambus Litho, East Kilbride, Glasgow.

Boxtree Limited
Broadwall House
21 Broadwall
London
SE1 9PL

A CIP catalogue entry for this book is available from the British Library.

ISBN 1 85283 839 6

Front cover photograph by Dave Hogan

Acknowledgements :

Many people have been extremely helpful in the making of this book. I would like to thank Loretta de Souza at RCA Records for her picture and information research; my sister, Charlotte Tomlinson, for her painstaking transcriptions of interviews; Claudia Connell for her tireless work against an ever-pressing deadline; Nigel-Martin Smith for asking me to write the book; Take That for being such excellent subjects; Dave Hogan for his brilliant pictures, and finally my wife Marion for putting up with long hours on the word processor and some very bad moods.

CONTENTS

Gary Barlow

FAMILY:

I was born on 20 January 1971, at home in Frodsham, Cheshire. My parents are Marjorie and Colin Barlow. I couldn't have wished for a better mother and father really. They've been married twenty-five years and never had a cross word to say to each other. Their relationship has made me look forward to the day when I can get married and have kids.

Dad used to be a product manager at United Kingdom Fertilisers but he retired about five or six years ago. Mum has been a science technician at Frodsham High School for years. It was my old school and it was an odd experience having your mother there all day. Whenever I stepped out of line the teachers would say, 'Gary, we'll send you to your mum.'

Mum's been a great support to me over the years; she's the backbone of the family, the boss. Like any mother, she is very proud of me. But my success hasn't come as a massive surprise to her. She always had confidence in me. If anyone ever asks mum if she thought this would happen to her boy, she always says 'Yes'. Mind you, she was knocked out when she saw us in concert for the first time. I don't think she realised how big it all was. She was totally flabbergasted!

My parents were responsible for my getting into music. When I was eleven, they asked me at Christmas if I wanted a keyboard or a BMX bike. I chose a keyboard and within about two weeks, I'd done everything this keyboard could do. So my dad said I obviously had a bit of talent for playing it, and he sold all his days off at work to buy me an organ. It cost him £600, which was a lot of money then. It was enormous, it virtually filled my bedroom; I started playing straight away and within about six months I was really good.

What a bonny baby...

Aged 3 years

Aged 4½ years

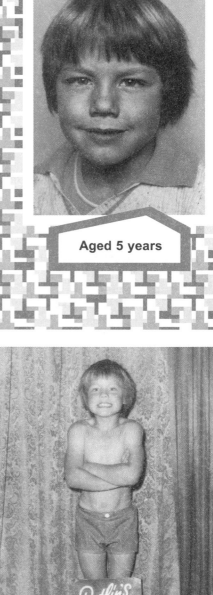

Aged 5 years

That was the start of my obsession with music I suppose. I always dreamed of being a pop star, like a lot of kids do. I loved Adam Ant and admired him for writing his own songs when everyone thought he was a manufactured star. I formed a mini-band at school based on him and the Ants; it was great fun bashing away on old biscuit tins making that drumming sound he used.

I moved out of home last year and bought my own place in Cheshire. It's a three-bedroom bungalow with a studio at the back of the house. It was my reward to myself when Take That took off; I bought an Escort Diesel too.

I have one brother, Ian. He's twenty-five years old and a self-employed builder with his own company in Frodsham. Ian still lives with my parents but he's recently got engaged to his girlfriend Julie, so he'll be on his way soon as well. It hasn't been easy for Ian, he's had to work really hard at his career. While I was earning all that money, he was on a YTS scheme and wasn't able to get a job at the end of it. For a year he tried to get a business going, but now he's doing well. He's a sensible bloke and he's drummed into me the need to be careful with money. I'm so careful now that the boys call me Ebeneezer Barlow. I am really, really tight with my money! I'm good with paying bills and saving and that's down to Ian and my mum.

My family are all very encouraging to me but I think mum is starting to find the fame thing a bit tiring. She gets so many people coming up asking for my autograph, it drives her mad. I think my family are very proud of me although they don't admit it very often. Mum always says to her friends that she wanted me to work in a bank or be a policeman. But she knew music was my real love and wanted me to do what I wanted.

Only third place Gary?

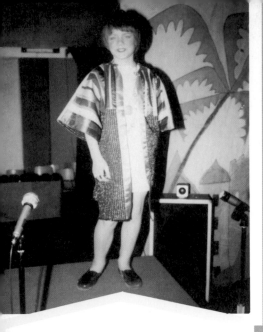

Aged 12, in Joseph and the Amazing Technicolor Dreamcoat

A cheeky 8-year-old

SCHOOL

"My first school was Weaver Vale in Frodsham. I was four years old when I went and ten when I left. My most vivid memory is playing Joseph in *Joseph And The Amazing Technicolor Dreamcoat* in my last year. I got the part because I was such a boisterous character and had a reasonably good voice then. From an early age I was a real entertainer. I'd do impressions of my neighbours, my friends and especially the teachers. At eleven, I moved on to Frodsham High School, where I ended up with six O levels in Music, Arts, Maths, English Language, Technical Drawing and Computer Studies. But by that time my mind was totally on music and I wasn't that interested in studies. The only reason I stuck with it is because the older guys I was playing with said I should, because music would never make me much money!"

Aged 11, in school uniform

Posing with his football in the front garden

9 years old but still clutching his teddy-bear

3

Gary was baring his torso for the camera from the age of 13 . . .

. . . but today he's often on the other side of the lens

WORK

"My school work always came second to my music. When I was ten I saw a talent competition in the Chester Chronicle which said: 'Conners Quay Labour Club presents Star 1984'. My mum took me down there. It was the full business with all the glitter and everything and I didn't even know what I was going to play.

My mum took me out to the car-park and told me a few jokes to say in between to chat to the crowd. She said to play 'A Whiter Shade of Pale'. I just went on like a cheeky little lad and I got through it - the audience loved it. At the end of the night the results came out and I came second. I was beaten by a duo - two lads. But Norman Hill, the secretary, came up to me and said 'Hey, listen, we've got a job here every Saturday night. We'll pay you £18.'- which was a lot of money then, especially for an eleven year-old! I thought great, I'm going to do it. And I did that for about a year.

Then I thought of doing a bit of freelance organ playing. In most clubs there are organists and drummers who get given the music five minutes before they go on to back the acts. So I busked around doing that for a year.

When I reached thirteen, I got friendly with this girl at school called Heather. We formed a duo together, doing the Carpenters and all that sort of stuff. She must have been the same age as me and we went down great in the clubs. For two years we played everything from clubs to old people's homes - anyone who would pay us. It was hard fitting my schoolwork in. My interest in studying got less and less.

When I was fourteen I thought: I've had enough of this on the road business, I want a residency, to play at one club every night and be in one place. A job came up at the Holton British Legion in Runcorn. It was four gigs a weekend, Friday night, Saturday night, Sunday dinner and Sunday night. My mum wasn't too happy at this point because it was a lot of hours what with school and everything. It was 8 pm to 2 am but it was a top club, and I would back people like Ken Dodd. I was on £140 a week at fourteen.

At fifteen my big chance come when Pebble Mill ran their school carol competition 'A Song for Christmas'. I wrote this song called 'Let's Pray For Christmas'.

My music teacher, Val Nelson, encouraged me to write a song for the contest. So I thought,

yeah I'm going to write a song. I went home and wrote it and it sounded quite good. So I called in my mum and said come and listen to this. She said, 'No, that's not right it's too miserable, too slow'. Mrs Nelson thought it was great and said she sent it off.

It was the longest two weeks of my life waiting for a reply. When it came I was in the gym climbing up the ropes. I saw Mrs Nelson come in and I knew what she was going to say. I walked up to her and said 'I've got it, haven't I?' and she said 'We're in!' Then she took me down to the headmaster's office. He was amazed. My mum came down from the science department and she was thrilled - she couldn't believe it.

The next two weeks were even longer. Pebble Mill invited me down to London to record the song at a place called West Heath Studios in West Hampstead. It was the first recording studio I'd ever been in. I met a guy called Bob Howes who said he'd record it in half an hour and I thought that was far too little time. But then I walked into the studio and there were thirty musicians. They all stood around with me in the middle, they stuck a pair of headphones on me and I was absolutely frightened to death. Then it was one, two, three, four and the orchestra struck up, and the sound was like no other. I don't think I've ever had a feeling like that since, all of a sudden all these guys were playing my song. I started singing and all these backing vocals came off these three girls and it was amazing. At the end all the violinists tapped their music stands with their fiddles to show their appreciation which was great. Then it was a case of waiting until it was filmed for TV.

I was desperate to do well. I won the semi-final, but, didn't win the final. But this guy Bob Howes took me aside and said he had never had a song written so well for this competition. He told me to carry on writing songs and to keep in touch with him. So off I went and wrote a load of stuff and sent it to him, and he invited me down to the studio again. He introduced me to a guy called Rod Argent who for the next two to three years was my contact. I used to send songs to him and he used to give me advice. He was my best influence. I did that until I was about seventeen. It was a really handy job because it gave me all week to write songs and stuff. And I was earning enough money to build up a big studio at home.

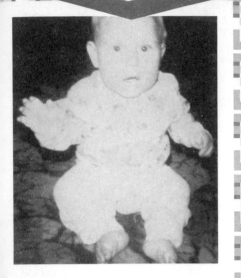

On the beach aged 2 ¹/₂.

MARK OWEN

FAMILY

" I was born on 27 January 1972, at our family's home in Oldham. My mum, Mary Frances Owen is thirty-nine years old but doesn't look it. She works as the supervisor at a bakery in Oldham. They make the cakes for people like Marks and Spencers. My sister Tracey works there too, but I don't know how long she will stay there. Tracey wants to be one of those people who jets away to the sun every summer and works in bars!

Mum enjoys her work; her friends don't understand why she still comes in when her son's a pop star, but she likes it. Though I don't think she would mind me saying she could stop! Mum's never expected any of what has gone on in my life, but she really enjoys it all and takes a real interest in what I do. She's a bit of a worrier like me and will say things like, 'Mark, what's happened to your new single? I haven't heard it on the radio yet.' When I buy new clothes she shakes her head and says she doesn't like them, but I know she does really.

I was always quite a good kid. The only real trouble I got into was when I was caught smoking. I was twelve and my friend made the mistake of writing me a letter saying, 'I'm not trying those ciggies again are you?' My mum found the letter and I got a real lecture for that.

Another bad thing I did was when I smacked a ball through our window while playing football with my younger brother, Daniel. Mum wasn't home so I tried to take the glass out and cut myself quite badly. I had to go hospital and have three stitches. She gave me a bigger telling off for that than the break itself.

Another time I broke my wrist playing basketball. By the time I got home from the game at 7pm on a Friday night, it was time for her to go to the Bingo hall. I said, 'Mum, my wrist is killing me, I think I need to go to the hospital.' But she told me to stop making a fuss and left me there for three hours in agony while she played bingo! She was horrified when she realised it was broken and she still is when I remind her about it now, which is quite often!

The worst thing mum's ever done to me is spraying my pet iguana, Nirvana, with what she thought was water while I was away. It was actually furniture polish. When I got back she was crying because she thought she'd killed him. But he was OK just a bit shiny!

My dad Keith used to be a decorator. Then he delivered wallpaper, and for the last six or seven years he has worked at a police station. We moved around a lot when I was a kid. Mum always wants to move; she doesn't like to stay in one place for too long. She's using the excuse of too many fans outside to try and persuade my dad to move again but he doesn't want to go. He reckons one day our house will be worth a lot of money as Mark Owens' Home! I don't get much chance to go home nowadays, just a few days every now and again. The phone calls cost a fortune, especially from Europe. My parents are still very happy together and we have never seemed to have many problems in our family. We are all quite close and talk about any problems we have. I've got a mellow, relaxed family and I'm very lucky. There are a few slammed doors every now and then, but my parents are there when I need them and I am there for them. When the band weren't taking off they were a great support.

My sister Tracey is eighteen and left school last year. I'm gutted actually because she's just passed her driving test before me. I can't believe it! I've got a car now, an old white X-reg Ford Fiesta, but I can't drive it. Tracey wants to be insured to drive it around - what a nightmare! Tracey thinks it is very funny what's happened to me. But she is proud of me, I think. We were both mad on Elvis Presley as kids: we used to brush our hair back, put on blue suede shoes and tight trousers and mimic The King to mum's Elvis records. I was hooked on performing from then on! My brother Daniel is taking his GCSEs this year. Our Daniel loves it most because there are girls outside our house all the time who are his age so they chase him instead of me now! He goes out with them all, they ignore me.

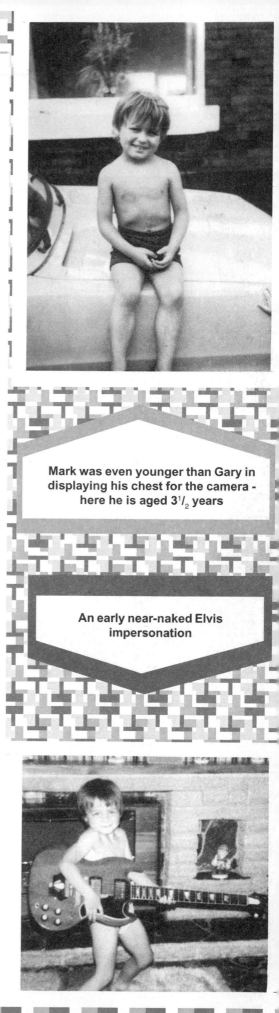

Mark was even younger than Gary in displaying his chest for the camera - here he is aged 3$\frac{1}{2}$ years

An early near-naked Elvis impersonation

Can you spot Mark? He's in the middle row, fourth from the right

Wearing more make-up than Kiss on a world tour, Mark is on the left

Snuggling up to a girl, aged 6

SCHOOL

My first school was a nursery called Havershaw School in Oldham. I remember crying on my first day and running up the street after mum dropped me off. The teachers had to drag me back! From the age of five until eleven, I went to the Holy Rosary Junior School. I was quickly into sports in a big way especially football and cross country. Every year there would be a huge sports day where all the schools in Oldham got together and competed. I took part in running and long jump and won the 100 metre sprint. I was so honest then I used to take the blame for things I didn't do, which wasn't too clever. I remember seeing this girl called Nicole Boswell put water into our sand pit one day and the teacher said none of us would get any milk until the culprit owned up. As no one owned up, I owned up for the class. What a mug! I was the only one that didn't get any milk!

I was in a lot of school plays. I remember playing the Little Drummer Boy in my junior school play and seeing my mum and dad in the audience they looked so proud with big smiles on their faces. I also played Jesus in my last year. It was the star role and I was chuffed. But my voice was beginning to break at the time and I could hear my speech getting deeper and deeper as it came up to the first night of the show. I was thinking, please don't break on stage. Luckily it held out. But soon afterwards it went and everyone would take the mickey out of me because I'd be coming out with these high pitched squeals. At eleven, I went to St Augustine's - a Catholic comprehensive. I was part of a group of lads who went around together playing football and break-dancing. I used to sit at the back of the class and have a laugh. We were quite a popular group. I was quite quiet and followed whatever the others did. We got on well with the teachers and didn't get up to too much trouble.

My favourite teacher was Mrs Proctor, who taught art. She was a really nice lady and I think I was one of her favourites. I used to sneak into extra lessons when I was supposed to be somewhere else. If I liked a subject I usually did quite well in it but I was never very good at revising. I always crammed everything into the last few days. My highest mark was 92 per cent in Maths. My lowest was 13 per cent in German. We used to go on school trips. The best one was to Majorca for a sporting holiday. One night we all chucked our trainers into the sea for a laugh, because if you didn't have trainers you couldn't wind surf and none of us liked it much. But the next day the Spanish bloke who ran the place came up and took us to his hut and there were all our trainers sitting there. He'd seen us chuck them into the water and gone and got them back. It was so embarrassing.

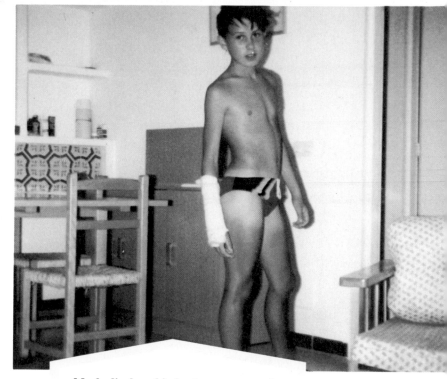

Mark displays his broken arm - and a lot more besides!

On the beach, again!

Mark's first passion was football. Here he is in the front row, second from the left

A handsome 16-year-old

Mark's bedroom at home

Relaxing after an exhausting phone-call

FOOTBALL

"I've been playing football seriously since I was twelve and I was hoping to become a professional footballer. The rest of the band call me Booter because I still play it all the time! I played right mid-field most of the time, and I've got more than twenty trophies stuffed in a cupboard somewhere.

I even had a trial for Manchester United. They came up to see me playing in a game for my local team, Hollingwood, and they were impressed enough to invite me down to play in a match between two teams of hopefuls. It was a nightmare - we got beat 14-1 and Ryan Giggs scored nine of them. Darren Ferguson played too and I had to mark him; he was bigger and faster and I never got near him! I had another trial with Huddersfield Town but I was quite badly injured at the time with my thigh which ruined it a bit. I had been waiting for this trial for four weeks so I played anyway. I just stood on the halfway line not being able to move my right leg for the whole game. When we finished they just said, 'Sorry but you are not really what we wanted.'

The best trial I had was with Rochdale. I went up there with a friend of mine and did a bit of training for about a week or two during the school holidays. They did actually say I could come up whenever I wanted but I never bothered going back up again. It was too much like hard work and made me realise I wouldn't be a footballer after all."

WORK

I finally left school at sixteen with six GCSEs in Art, English, Maths, RE, Physics and Economics.

I didn't really know what I wanted to be when I left school. I started by working in a clothes shop called Zuttis in Oldham. Then I got offered a job in Barclays Bank, Oldham, which I did for about two months. I met Gary at the time I was working in the bank.

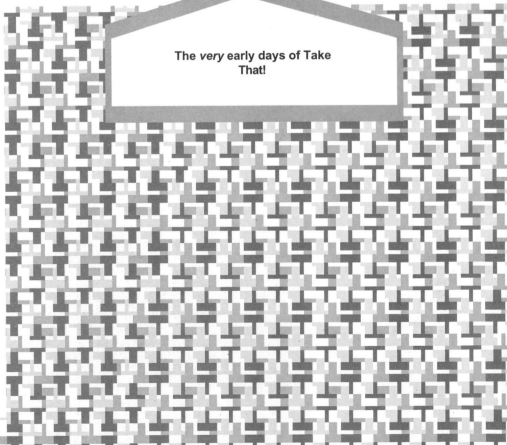

The *very* early days of Take That!

Mark today

Howard aged 1

A surprised Howard in the middle of brothers Colin and Michael

At a farm in Wales, aged 15 months

Howard with his mum and brothers at sister Samantha's christening

Aged 3 years, with brothers and Samantha

HOWARD DONALD

FAMILY

❝ I was born at home on 28 April, 1968, in Droylsden, Manchester at 8.30am. My mum, Kathleen, is a secretary at an infants school. She changed her name from Donald after divorcing my dad Keith and remarrying my stepdad Mike ten years ago. I was about eight years old when my parents got divorced. I can't really remember much about it. I went through a stage when I used to have lots of nightmares, which may have been a side effect of the divorce.

I still see my dad about once every two weeks. Everyone is still friends. He used to be a Latin American dance teacher and mum was a singer, so music is in the blood. Dad's a part-time caretaker in a school now. He got pestered to death at the old school he was working at, so he moved to a new one in Hyde. My dad loves it all and buys all the magazines and newspapers and everything.

Dad hasn't remarried but he's going out with someone. My parents get on really well and still exchange Christmas presents.

My first memory is playing Cowboys and Indians in this mate's back garden and I threw my gun at this lad behind a tree and it whacked him on the head so badly that there was blood everywhere. I ran home and hid in the bathroom pretending to clean my teeth for two hours. Then his parents turned up and I was terrified. But mum saw them off. She said I was a very good boy most of the time. But she didn't know most of what I was up to. I only told her a year ago that I skived off school for five weeks once. She never knew, and couldn't believe it.

When the band started, mum wasn't keen on it and wanted me to get a proper job. Now she can't believe it but she doesn't treat me any differently. I'm not a star at home that's for sure. She's happy to see me but she doesn't run out telling her friends. She's quite shy like me. I don't mind the fans being outside my home but my mother gets fed up having to get up every five minutes to open the door. It can get a bit irritating when they throw stones at the window and start shouting through the letter box. The gate is covered in graffiti, with loads of litter everywhere - I'm amazed the neighbours don't complain. However much money I get, mum will stay the same. If she won the pools she wouldn't change. She's a really nice lady.

I have three brothers Michael, twenty-eight, Colin, thirty-one, and Glenn, eleven. And I have a sister, Samantha, twenty-two. Michael is a body-builder - he fits boxes on the back of wagons in Shaw. Colin works for a double glazing company in Middleton, Glenn is about to go to secondary school and Samantha is a personal secretary in an office in Manchester. None of them is married.

My brother Colin's the most interested in what I do. If he get's on the phone to me you can't get him off. I love him for it but when he's phoning me every two minutes it's a bit painful!

Scaling the heights, aged 4 years

With Mum, brother and sister after mass on Sunday

Aged 7, with family at Blackpool

Visiting Santa with sister Samantha

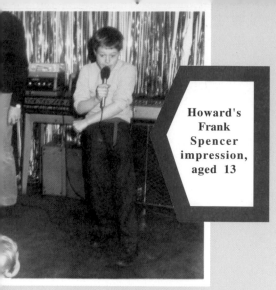

Howard's Frank Spencer impression, aged 13

At school, in the middle row, second from the left

Howard's pride and joy, aged 13 - his BMX bike

On the beach aged 16, with *very* blond hair!

SCHOOL

" My first school was Moreside Junior School in Jorsdan, Manchester. I was good in junior school unlike now! I was more into the way the system worked at the junior school. Things started to go wrong when I moved to secondary school, Little Moss High School for Boys.I left with just three GCSEs in English, Maths and Geography.

I wasn't that keen on school. I was more into being a fool and making people laugh, I think that's what I do best. I was a bit of a class joker, throwing things around the room, throwing things at other people. I was always at the front so the teacher could keep an eye on me. But a lot of the time I used to bunk off and go into the meadows near the school.

I once stayed off school for five weeks. I only intended having a couple of days off but I enjoyed it so much that I kept having another day, and then another. I used to lie in meadows and hang around, anything so long as it wasn't on my mum's shopping route.But as soon as I was found out I got the cane.

I wasn't that bad really. I was BMX mad, breakdance mad, very short and had a side parting hairstyle at thirteen.

My hair was much lighter and I wasn't interested in girls much then. In my third year I really fancied a teacher at school but she didn't notice me which broke my heart.At thirteen I wanted to be an airline pilot, but now I want to keep pumping out records and get to as many territories as we can. When I left school at 16, I did a YTS scheme job with a vehicle painters firm called Knibbs in Manchester. At the end of my training scheme I went out looking for something and ended up joining a firm called Wimpole Garages. My job entailed restoring vehicles, doing a bit of spot painting on cars and fitting wings to them. I was with Wimpole for about two years and I still go back and see the lads to show them how down to earth I still am! They give me a hard time, then ask me to sign their daughters' posters. I wouldn't miss one minute of it. I love what I do now. It's not the money, the girls, or the limos, it's the performing and the fans. "

Far better being a natural brunette!

jason orange

FAMILY

> I was born at 7.30am on 10 July, 1970, at Crumpsall Hospital in Manchester, twenty minutes before my twin brother Justin.

Justin is one of my five brothers and now works in a Manchester nightclub as Assistant Manager. Just is engaged to a girl called Lisa, but there is no date for the wedding yet. Girl-wise he was always miles ahead of me but I was the one who looked after him. Hc used to get into fights and I used to bail him out. I once got called into the headmaster's office because of something Justin had done. But instead of saying so, I stood there and took the blame. At school we were known as the Terrible Twosome. If one was off ill, the other would go sick too so the ill one wouldn't be left on his own. I supported Manchester United and he supported City so there was always a lot of friendly rivalry. We do know each other very well, like most twins I suppose. If Justin's upset about something, I can tell before anyone else. I live with my brother Simon. He's twenty-five, and a financial salesman selling pensions and stuff like that. He was married at nineteen and divorced at twenty-one and has a lovely little daughter called Stephanie. Dominic is nineteen and a painter and decorator. He works for the same local firm that I used to work for. Samuel is fourteen and still at school. He reads all the magazine articles about me and is dead proud. He's my little buddy.

And Oliver is the youngest, he's just eleven years old.

I'm close to all my brothers. We all give each other support. We used to argue a lot as brothers do, but none of us were ever young ruffians. We didn't have much money when we were

Jason aged10 months with his twin brother Justin and older brother Simon

Jason's fashion sense was pretty well defined even at the age of 2 years!

If Jason were to do this with his friends now, he'd make the 10 o'clock news!

At school - Jason and Justin in matching outfits in the back row

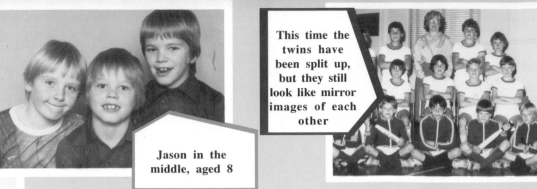

Jason in the middle, aged 8

This time the twins have been split up, but they still look like mirror images of each other

Jason and Justin aged 11. Jason always wore red because he supported Manchester United. Brother Justin supported City

Jason on holiday with his mum and younger brother Oliver

Jason breakdancing, aged 13

young. But mum did her best - and we were always happy.

My mother's name is Jennifer. My dad, Anthony, has two daughters from a new marriage. I don't see much of him though. I look back and see how he left my mum with us kids and it hurts when I think back to that. When I see him it's like: 'Hi Dad, how are you doing?' and 'Hi son, how are you doing?' and we chat. It's not really a father and son relationship but it's OK. My parents' divorce was the saddest thing that has ever happened to me. Myself and my brothers were all affected in different ways. It was very traumatic for everyone involved. When dad left, we all stayed with mum. I'm very proud of mum because she did a great job in bringing us all up. I know how hard it is looking after myself now, let alone five others. She was incredible. I call her a lot to see how she is, and I love and respect her very much.

I used to get mum into trouble a few times. Once she was chatting to someone in a shopping precinct and this friend jokingly said 'now no shoplifting Jenny'. When we entered another shop a few minutes later I shouted out, 'Mum, are you going to steal things in here like you said you were?' She was so embarrassed she says she wished the ground had opened up and swallowed her. She doesn't mention things she wants in front of me because she knows I'll go out and buy them for her.

Mum loves the success we have had. She has a part-time job in the doctor's surgery. I am proud of the fact that she is proud of me. My ambition is to buy her a big house; that would be great.

Jason with his brother Samuel

A change of image, Jason & Justin dressed up as the Krays at a fancy dress party

Jason with his best mate Neil

SCHOOL

" My first school was Havely Hey School in Wythenshawe, Manchester. That was my nursery, infants and junior school. Then I moved on to South Manchester High School. I left there at sixteen with not many qualifications. School didn't hold much interest for me. We didn't get to learn anything because of the teacher strikes. I was into sports I used to enjoy football, running, swimming.

I didn't get into trouble at school, but I used to bunk off and got a few detentions. I was always quite shy at school approaching anyone from teachers to girls was a nightmare for me. I hardly said a word in class, never joined in any discussions or anything like that. It's taken a long time for me to come out of my shell but I am much happier and more confident now. But school didn't have much to offer when I was there.

My last day at school was great. I walked out of those gates and turned round to look at my old school and thought 'Freedom!' "

No, it's not a pretty fan who's gone backstage - it's Jason's mum!

WORK

" We got jobs on a YTS scheme. I applied for decorating and Justin applied for plumbing. All my mates applied for joining or plumbing or what ever. My first firm was a painting and decorating company called Direct Works. I did a year's YTS and then I took an exam and got taken on as a full time apprentice for four years. I still keep in touch with a guy called Ray Smith who I worked with at that time. I was quite lucky because he was a brilliant tradesman and he taught me the job really well.

I enjoyed the work and loved learning the trade. A lot of the people I worked with just used to moan about their wives and kids and how much bonus they didn't get at the end of the work and in the end I found it all rather demoralising. It got a bit depressing to go to work sometimes and when the band started gaining my interest more and more, I just knew I didn't want to spend the rest of my life working there. I wanted to get out. "

Jason (left) with his mates, Neil and Simon, on Christmas day 1984

Jason with his mates, in a local pub

26

Robbie at 6 months with his big sister, Sally

Aged 2 with his grandad, Jack

Robbie singing *Summer Nights* at a talent competition in Spain. He won first prize!

A young mountaineer, aged 4

ROBBiE WiLLiaMS

FAMILY

" I was born on 13 February 1974, at The Royal Infirmary in Newcastle under Lyme. I have a sister called Sally who is twenty-eight. She's a florist in Newcastle, she's single and doesn't have any kids.

We were living in a pub called The Red Lion next to the Port Vale football ground when I was born. I've supported them ever since, through thick and thin. Then we moved to Stoke, where I am now.

My mum and dad are divorced, they split up when I was three and it didn't have any effect on me as I've always been loopy. Neither has remarried and I doubt they will. I have a very good relationship with both of them. We wouldn't have had it any other way. I see a lot of relationships between father and son/daughter disintegrate and I think, thank God that ain't me. It had its advantages too. When I was growing up, I'd see a few of my friends getting told off by their dad and then their mum. And I'd be thinking, well, if I get told off by my mother I can go and tell my dad. And if I get told off by my dad I can go and say, 'Mum, me dad's been telling me off'. It has had some effect on my attitude towards marriage I suppose. If I do get married I'm going to wait until I'm in my late thirties at least.

My dad is a well-known comedian called Pete Conway who made the final of *New Faces* in 1974. Now he is an entertainments manager on holiday camps in places like Scarborough and Great Yarmouth. I used to go and see him every summer and spend six weeks or so with him.

Mum, whose full name is Teresa Jeanette Williams, likes to think that she's forty... but I'm not convinced about that. My first memories are of her making me wear a daft romper suit

Posing in the back garden, aged 8

In amateur dramatics, aged 12

Robbie as the Artful Dodger in the local theatre society production of *Oliver!*

Robbie with his mum and sister, Sally

Robbie with his idol, Brian Robson, at Haydock Park

with a yellow canary on it. My mum used to run a pub and I remember her making me sit there in full view of everyone wearing this horrible thing.

I used to have a fetish for chucking things out of the window. One Saturday I got all the takings out of the pub till, about £2000, and threw it out of the window. It went all over the place and mum went spare.

Another time I threw all her bras and knickers out on to the heads of mounted policemen below who were trying to control the football crowd outside. You can imagine how they felt. Mum was so embarrassed she could hardly look.

But mum used to get her own back with all the clothes she used to put me in. The other day I saw pictures of me at my cousin Jane's wedding when I was about six. Mum had me dressed up in these chequered tartan flares and wide collar bigger than my head. What a nightmare.

But mum was great to me and she's over the moon now about my success. The best thing is that she never talks about me to anyone except her close friends and my sister. And she doesn't ask me for autographs for her friends all the time. You need to be able to go home and escape from all that occasionally.

Mum helped me out all the time when I was trying to get into acting and music. She used to pay for me to come from Stoke to Manchester. When the band started it cost £8 a day by train and sometimes it was five times a week. It's nice to treat her now I can afford to. Mum still runs a flower shop and a dress shop and is very happy.

Robbie on holiday in Spain, after his
first tasting of beer!

SCHOOL

My first school was Dolly's Lane School near my house in Stoke.

My first day at school I saw all these kids crying as they said goodbye to their mums, but I was more concerned with playing with the lads. I told mum to go home; she was more upset than I was!

After that, Millhill Primary School. I can remember going on camp to Wales and I had a tenner to spend on the last day and I thought I was a millionaire. After that I went onto St Margaret Ward, which was the local High School. I was there until sixteen and ended up with eight or nine GCSEs. I was a good lad at school in that I never got caught. I did the normal laddish stuff that you'd expect a fourteen year old to get up to. We used to go out at dinner time. I didn't smoke, but I'd go to smokers' corner. And you weren't allowed to wear trainers, so I'd always put them on. I always used to be the one that would make the class laugh. Our set always made the class laugh, but as soon as we'd done it and the teacher would turn round, we'd sit straight and the rest would be laughing and they'd get told off.

I used to perform at the Theatre Royal in Stoke on Trent. I was in *Oliver Twist, Chitty Chitty Bang Bang, Pickwick, Fiddler on the Roof, The King and I, Hans Christian Anderson* and a few more. My favourite was *Oliver Twist,* I played the Artful Dodger, which was pretty true to my character. I didn't have any formal acting training. I don't really know how I got into it, I just found myself at an audition one day. Hans Christian Anderson was my first one. I can remember the first night that I performed because I peed in my pants. I was eleven years old and terrified. Nobody noticed, not even my mum.

I joined the band in the middle of my going from school to college. In fact I'm still registered at the Sixth Form College at St Margaret's Ward now. When I go in next time I'll probably get detention for being three years late.

Aged 15, in a school
photo

JOBS

 When I left school at sixteen I wanted to be an actor. But my first job was selling double-glazing with a few local firms. My sister's boyfriend was the owner of one, so I went and canvassed for them for a while. I did that for three months and found it utterly soul destroying.

I used to have to go round to people's houses trying to flog them double-glazing. They'd say, 'Come in for a second, give me a quote and then leave.' But once inside you stay there as long as you can. You don't leave that house until they sign for those windows. But I find it difficult to be dishonest to people so I used to tell them that the windows were overpriced and leave. As you can imagine I was never very good at it.

HOW THEY MET

As we know and love them now, but before. . .

MARK'S STORY

The first member of the band I met was Gary, at a studio in Manchester. My sister knew some guy who was a keyboard player and he used to go up to the studios with his band. So I asked if there was any chance of me going along with them and helping out. I was a tea-boy really, literally making teas. Gary came in one night and we started talking and got to be good mates.

After a while I started going down to Gary's house. He was recording his own stuff at home and asked me to do some backing vocals and simple things like that. He was doing a lot of gigs at the time, so I'd go to the gigs with him and carry his stuff and just help him out. We formed a band called Cutest Rush, with me singing his songs. But it was never that serious.

Then someone suggested we see Nigel Martin Smith and try to get him to manage us. Jason and Howard had been in to see him as well and he introduced us all with a mind to us getting together in a band. My first impressions of them were good. I remember seeing Jason dancing and I thought, oh my God, he's brilliant! I tried to breakdance and they fell about laughing. But I got the hang of it slowly.

Then we got Robbie. We put an advertisement in the paper for a fifth member. We did a song called *Girl*, which Gary had written; Billy Ocean's hit *Girl of My Dreams*, *Get Off My Cloud* by the Rolling Stones; *Waiting Around* which is on the B side of *Do What Like You Like;* and *A Million Love Songs*.

For the first year of the band things moved so slowly that I was still doing some engineering for a mate on the side. Nigel had gone to all the record companies and it got really disappointing when we just heard no, no, no all the time. Then we decided that we ought to go on our own. So we released our first single on Nigel's own label - Dance UK.

When we released our first record *Do What U Like* it was very exciting. I think we went in the charts at about No 87. But it got us noticed and more and more people were beginning to show an interest in us.

We signed up to RCA Records in about September, 1991 that was a brilliant moment. After signing the deal I remember the first night we came to London. We came down by plane and there was a limousine to pick us up. We were all looking at each other and couldn't believe it.

We released the second single *Promises* and it made the chart, entering at No 38. We were in the Regency Hotel in London at the time and we were so chuffed that Howard went through the bed because we were jumping up and down so much. The next week we dropped to 40 and we were a bit upset about that.

But we went ahead with a third single, *Once You've Tasted Love*, and hoped that would be a big hit. It wasn't. It got to No 45 and that was it. That was a really bad moment. We didn't feel like packing it yet because we enjoyed it. But we were worried as to whether the record company or press would keep on our side. They stood by us which was great.

We decided to go on a massive tour of schools called The Big Schools Tour. We were doing three schools

Take That in the days before Marky Mark had ever even thought of dropping his trousers to display his boxers. . .

during the day and two clubs in the evening. I remember setting a target of 50,000 people seeing us by the time the next single came out and we did achieve it. Our hard work paid off when we released a cover version of the old hit *It Only Takes a Minute* and it went in at No 16. We were in a restaurant called La Reserve in Fulham and all the fans were outside crying. It was fantastic - we felt we had finally cracked it. The record climbed and climbed until it got to No 7. We did *Top of The Pops* after that which was like a dream come true.

By now things were going very fast and the next single *I Found Heaven* was another success reaching No 15. We were all excited about shooting the video because we were told we would be doing it on a beach somewhere and we were all having these visions of it being in Spain or Greece. We ended up going to the Isle of Wight where it was bloody freezing. It was windy and cold and there we were dancing in the sea.

When our album *Take That And Party* shot into the charts at No 5 we all celebrated with a big party. Our next single *A Million Love Songs* got to No 7. It sent the album right back up again to No 2 and the video was No 1 for fourteen weeks. It was one of Gary's songs and showed that the band had a bit more talent - it proved that we didn't just do dance songs. We released *Could It Be Magic* for Christmas and it was our biggest hit - reaching No 3 and staying in the top five all over the festive period. We were all thrilled because the only people between us and No 1 were big overseas acts like Whitney Houston and Michael Jackson. The next single was *Why Can't I Wake Up With You* which went to No 2. Now we are looking forward to the rest!

ROBBIE'S STORY

When I left school, I thought, right, I've got no qualifications, I'll go out and see what I can do for myself. My mother heard about this audition for a band in a local paper and told me to go along for it, so I did. I went along to Nigel's offices and all the others were sitting there. I remember thinking what a weird bunch of lads they were, and really didn't think we could ever be a band. At the beginning I thought Gary was boring - he was really hard to get to know and he wasn't letting anybody inside his mind. Mark was little and cute and grinned an awful lot. He had a mop of hair and looked very trendy. He obviously spent a lot of money on clothes. Jason, I looked up to because he'd been on the TV and danced brilliantly. As for Howard, I can't really remember thinking about him much. For my audition I had to sing a song from *Joseph And The Amazing Technicolor Dreamcoat*. At the end they said they'd let me know but it was about three or four weeks before they told me. Then they just rang me and said I'd got it. I was over the moon. By this time I did actually think that they were going to be successful. I was scared of Nigel at first. I'd never heard of him before, but everyone else had and he seemed to have a lot of authority. He'd been and seen and done everything.

The first time I got together with the band was very soon after the phone call. I received this letter through the post saying, 'This is where you've got to go, this is what you've got to do, these are the numbers you will be rehearsing ...' So I turned up at the studio and we rehearsed all the numbers and I was terrible: I didn't dance well and kept getting everything wrong. The others were excellent, they all knew the steps and everything. But I slowly got the hang of it and caught up with them. The first proper gig was at Flicks nightclub in Huddersfield in front of about 30 people. It was awful. Our first real TV show was *The Hit Man And Her* show hosted by Pete Waterman and Michaela Strachan. It was about two months into the band and should have been nerve racking but it wasn't really for me. I just went on and went to work.

HOWARD'S STORY

I met Jason at this club called the Apollo in Manchester where we used to go breakdancing all the time. I was about seventeen then. I used to watch him dance and I used to think 'God I wish I could break dance like him'. We got talking and got on really well. We didn't think of making anything big. We just got together and started making routines together. I first met Nigel in his office. Jay already knew Nigel and he took me along to see him, which is where we first met Mark and Gary. I hadn't really heard of Nigel beforehand. I knew he managed lots of big acts and that he was a really big manager. We sat down and had a good meeting with Mark and Gary. My first impressions of Gary and Mark were good.

Mark's all smiles so we instantly took to Mark, but Gary was a bit quiet and reserved at first. The next step was to get a fifth member, which was Robbie. Our first gig at Flicks was very interesting. We were all a bit gutted at the lack of people though I didn't expect more than a hundred because we were just nobodies at the time. But we ended up really enjoying it because we could make mistakes and it didn't matter. It was our first gig and we had done it. We were happy because we performed well even if there was hardly anyone there.

It just started picking up more after that, different clubs, different places. I remember one gig in particular during the first year. It was an outdoor gig in Stoke on a wooden floor placed on the grass. It was chucking it down with rain and me and Jason had to do some breakdancing. We went running out, slipped on our bums and went all over the show. We were laughing so much as we lay there that we couldn't get up and do the routine. It was hilarious.

JASON'S STORY

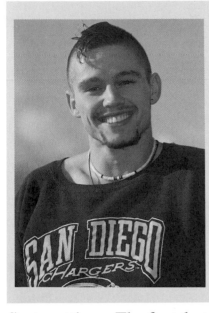

My first impression of the band when I was first met them was great. I remember first meeting Gaz. He came confidently through the door and came over as really pleasant. I remember thinking how cute Marky was, he just smiled all the time. I had good impressions of every one of them when I first met them. The fact that very few people turned up to the first gig at Flicks didn't really matter. We were there on stage performing in front of 30 people and that was good enough for me. I think we got paid about £20, enough for a Kentucky Fried Chicken, each. But it was really exciting and nerve racking at the same time. I wasn't even thinking about record companies it was just like, so what, I'm having a good time with the boys. However, it did eventually become demoralising not to have instant successes. When the first two singles didn't do anything we were really upset. I don't think you can expect anything in this business and it taught us to just take everything as it comes. I think now that because we've had two flops, it's kept our feet firmly on the ground. I think it was a good lesson. Having our first hit with *Promises* felt amazing. But the biggest thrill came with *it Only Takes a Minute*. We worked so hard on promoting that record that when it did finally come through it was incredible. We were on such a high. Whilst doing a signing session I was thinking about my family and friends, hoping they were listening to the charts. It was a brilliant feeling.

Anyone for a haircut?

Striking a pose even Madonna couldn't copy!

GARY'S STORY

All I really ever wanted was a record deal and to be famous. After a couple of years of playing in clubs, being approached by dodgy managers offering dodgy deals, I finally met up with Nigel, who from the start was very straight with me. He said he was getting a band together and was very interested in my songs. When I went into the office, Nigel introduced me to Jason and Howard. Nigel said he was looking for dancers and singers and asked if I knew anyone and I immediatly thought of Mark who I had met a few months earlier. So I phoned him up and he immediately came around. But Nigel was the force behind it all. He told us that we had to really work if we wanted a record deal. We weren't much of an outfit for the first six months. We had been put together and told to get on with it but it wasn't easy because we didn't know each other. Slowly we got it together - and it became more and more fun. We weren't having hit records but we were having a good time, getting our name around and being recognised. It was our first TV appearance on *Cool Cube*, the satellite show, that turned things around for us. I wrote a couple of songs called *Waiting Around* and *Girl* for it and then we devised two dance routines to go with it which Nigel liked. We did well enough to get on to *The Hitman And Her* show and then all of sudden things took off and people became interested in us. The schools tour helped even more. We loaded up the car with speakers, amps, tape, tape decks and microphones and went to the schools to meet our fans. They opened up to us and it worked brilliantly.Now, when we go on tour, the feelings are still the same: we aim to have a good time and I think we give our fans a good

time too. I hope when people go to the concerts they come out with a smile on their faces.

All I want is for the band to be as good on stage as we are in the studio. We're constantly growing and doing new things, but most importantly I think the five of us are now better friends than we ever were.

GiRLS GiRLS GiRLS

ROBBIE

> My first kiss was in a boiler closet when I was about six. The girl's father was in the front room next door and we thought that was dead good because he could have caught us. I recently found out that the girl concerned is now pregnant at sixteen which was quite a shock. I'm not the father though; I only kissed her. . .

The girls used to think I was cute when I was very young because I was this chubby little guy who went around pulling faces and cracking jokes. I hated being called cute. There was nothing worse than hearing some girl I fancied saying I was really cute. I'd be devastated because I wanted to be hunky and fanciable anything but cute. I did have a lot of spots so maybe I was lucky to be called cute at all! The first girl to send me a Valentine's card was called Lisa. I don't get any now of course.

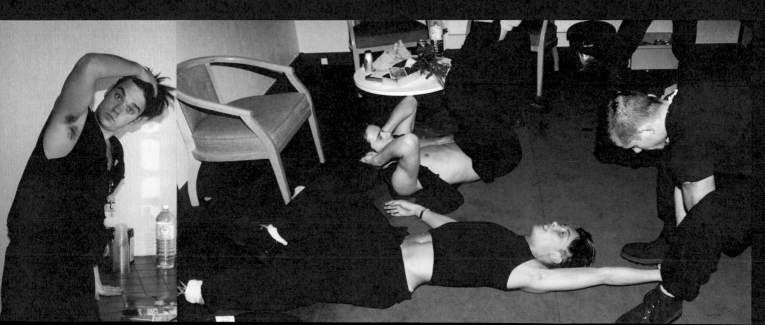

I've never had a serious relationship. I've had loads of girlfriends but they've been for two to three weeks. I want to know what a serious relationship is about. I'm still at the stage where I see three a month - nothing serious. People ask me what my idea of love is and I have no idea. Although I've never been in love I have been infatuated a few times and had my heart broken. I've always been shy when it comes to girls and I think humour is something you can hide behind.

 If I went on from school to go to sixth form college there would be no ways girls would be throwing themselves at me. Just because you're in there and you're in the press, on the television and everything, they look up to you. I used to go to discos and clubs and things when I was younger and at the end of the night I'd go over a girl and say, 'Do you fancy a dance?' and she'd say 'No.' Now it's my turn. All these girls are giving it the 'Robbie, Robbie, Robbie please dance with me.' And I just play it really cool and say 'No, no, no.' Girls get so desperate that they write to my mum or my nan and say how much they love them and how wonderful they are. And at the end of all that they add and your son's not bad either, any chance of arranging a meeting. . . I haven't got time for a relationship. My mum, sister and gran give me a lot of love but I miss a girl/boyfriend relationship. My nan Bee Williams gets really emotional. If she could wrap me in a ball of cotton-wool she would. When she first saw my picture in the papers she got all tearful. But she still thinks I'm about eight. If I go home she says things like, 'Have you been to the toilet?' When my mum goes away and I'm in the house by myself, nan says: 'You must come up tomorrow and I'll cook you something.'

JASON:

“ My first kiss was with a girl called Karen when I was twelve It happened in my garden and she brought her dog with her. Karen is my mate Neil's sister. She's my age and we'd known each other a long time before we kissed. It was pretty atrocious, a really bad performance on my part. I was so anxious to get my first snog out of the way that I just grabbed her. But her stupid dog jumped up and pawed me against a wall and she ran off. I'm glad she never told anyone how bad it was because all the other girls would have stayed well away from me. We haven't really spoken about it since, though I mentioned it once in an interview and she was chuffed! She's got a boyfriend and a baby now.

When I was thirteen I felt vastly inferior to a lot of my friends because they all said they had lost their virginity when of course they hadn't. As it happened things worked out well for me because I met a girl I really loved and when we did lose our virginity it was dead nice. I believe the right time for sex is when you are ready for it. You should never do anything because all your mates tell you to. And never forget precautions when you do meet the person you want to make love with. In an ideal world everyone would kiss, hug, have a baby and live happily ever after, but life isn't like that. I love girls. I can look at them and always find something attractive.I like flirting as long as it is done in a humorous way. I enoy being the centre of attention and having a laugh with girls. But it's just a game really, if you can cheer someone up by flirting with them then why not?

I get a lot closer to a girl than a lad. They are a lot more sensitive, more willing to listen and open up to you. I like dark, prominent features rather than perfectly set features. And I like confident girls but not show-offs. I will marry someone because of who they are, not what they look like.

As we become more famous we won't be sure of any girl's intentions. We are always going to be wondering does this person really want to be my friend or have they got a dictaphone in their pockets? Mark and Robbie take care of all the female adoration so the pressure's off me. I still get some of course. It's a real good feeling but you have to learn how to handle it. Normally we're in the place, do a show and then we're out. There are always kids trying to get into our hotel but we've got minders and all that.

GARY

" My first kiss was with a girl called Melanie Garnett. I was about eight at the time and we had quite a steady relationship for about four years. The kiss came at her seventh birthday party. I was totally in love and we taught each other how to kiss.

When I was eleven a girl called Julie broke my heart. We were both in the same panto and went out for a month. Then she finished with me. I think I've broken hearts but I'm still friends with my ex-girlfriends.

Heather was my long-time partner and the love of my life and I stayed with her for about five years. I was very romantic I remember one Christmas making up this huge box of presents for her. I filled it with a gold chain, a watch with her name on it and a cuddly toy, everything a girl could possibly dream of from a boyfriend. It was great watching her face when she opened it. We split up when I was about seventeen though our relationship really finished when we were fourteen or fifteen. We were really good friends so it carried on a bit. I do still see her occasionally, but she's moved away to university.

Honesty is always the best policy in relationships. If ever there is a problem in relationships it's usually because of a lack of communication. Arguments start and are never resolved because couples don't talk to each other. If you think about it, you can get through anything by sitting down quietly and discussing things. And if you don't agree, then you must go your separate ways.

About a year after Heather and I broke up I started going out with a girl called Nicky from Runcorn. I was earning big money by now, and she was the sort of girl a rock star should have: mini skirt, blonde hair, the business. She was about sixteen and I was eighteen and we hit it off really well. I've always been one for long-term relationships and this was one of those where where you start seeing them every night: it was the last Rolo business. Nicky would come and load the speakers into the car and generally help out. But when the band started Nigel wasn't keen on us having girlfriends because of all the problems it would cause later on. Although he was right, none of us really listened to him at the beginning, and then as we started spending more and more time away and all the fans began chasing us, the cracks started to happen in our relationships.

Now we are successful, we are all quite aware that there will be plenty of offers when we go on the road and there are. But I am not that tempted really. I can honestly swear on my life that I've never had a one night stand in my life and I'm proud of it. I think if we were a band like Bon Jovi it would be expected as part of our job. But I am proud of the image we've got for ourselves.

My mates are all amazed when I go home, they say things like, 'God you must have birds hanging off the roof.' But basically it's the complete opposite. It is tempting when you're signing autographs and some gorgeous girl says she wants your body. It's really hard to say no. But however tempting, at the end of the day you have to ask yourself what are you in it for. I think I'm in it to write music and to sing in front of audiences. **"**

HOWARD

"My first girlfriend was when I was eleven years old. I saw her just before Christmas and said hello to her. I'm sure she remembers me, she's probably sick of seeing me on TV. It was nothing serious, I thought I was in love but I really wasn't. She was the first girl I kissed, though I'm not sure if she knows that. Our first snog wasn't much of a snog really it was more of a peck. I'd learned how to do it in a Truth or Dare game.

I had a serious relationship which broke up about three months into the band. I was so busy with the band that I couldn't carry it on. I just couldn't cope with going away and that was for only a week. I was quite cut up by that. I've seen her a few times because she's the sister of my friend. She's engaged now so I've got no chance!

We get tons of letters, marriage proposals, and even knickers every week. I used to write love letters myself at school to teachers I fancied. I like the amount of effort the fans put into drawings of us, portraits, the simplest of things is the nicest. Sometimes when I come home I wish the fans would give us a bit of peace. Some can spoil it for others by throwing things and in that way it gets my parents angry and then it gets me angry.

I wish I had time for romance now but I don't meet anyone. I ask my sister to bring her friends round but she won't. In a woman I look for the hair first, but personality has to be the major thing. I find it very difficult now because some girls pretend that they don't know you so they can go out with you, when really they do know you.

I would describe myself as sensitive, disorganised, caring, sporty, shy, modest, romantic but I think I've lost it a bit now. I miss that. There's a lot of times when I wish I had a girlfriend but it's a no-go area. Because I want to do as well as I can in my career. I like the girls. I don't take advantage of them. It's not good to get involved because you can't hold a steady relationship down.

I was quite successful with the girls before Take That, but I've never been like a flirt with different girls every night. I got a lot of people telling me that I was good looking and I'm the sort of person that goes red and embarrassed if someone tells me that.

It's weird to think that three years ago you weren't anything and all of a sudden there's so many girls that want you.

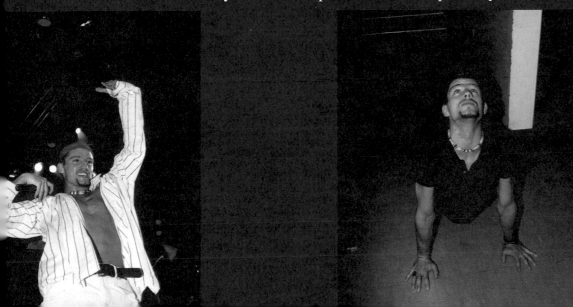

MARK

" The first girl I really fancied was my babysitter Jackie. I couldn't wait for her to come round and look after us, but her boyfriend used to tag along too.

My first kiss was when I was playing a game of Truth or Dare with about ten friends of mine when I was nine. My dare was to kiss one of the girls called Michelle in front of everyone. I was always a bit slow with girls and didn't actually have a girlfriend until I was thirteen. My younger brother Daniel had girls from the age of seven!

My first proper girlfriend was called Wendy and we went out together for three weeks. She had the daftest laugh I have ever heard and when she erupted I used to cringe!

At junior school I fancied this girl called Lisa. On Valentine's Day I brought her a little gold chain but nothing came of it. She ended up going out with my best mate - I was gutted. In fact I still need to get my own back for that one....

I never used to brag about girls to my mates because I think that is really rotten. I have more respect for girls than that. Anyway in my school it was usually the girls who used to brag about how far they had gone with us lads. I'd hear these rumours about myself and say: 'I never did that. She's lying.' No-one would believe me of course. When I was in the second year I used to try and get the sixth form girls. There was one I fancied rotten called Tracey and I remember one Christmas I chased her around the corridors with mistletoe. She locked herself in the ladies loo until I gave up. She did let me walk home with her once though and she drank some of my Coke. I kept the can on top of my TV for two years!

Even then girls used to call me cute and I hate that. My mum has even started saying it. It's only because I am small, if I was 6ft no-one would say anything because I'd batter them.

I went through one stage at school where I was going out with the same girl for six to eight months. It was towards the end of my schooldays and I lost contact with a lot of mates because of it. That was a big mistake. Come Friday night I would say, 'Oh no, I'm seeing my girlfriend.' In the end we finished because we got bored with each other now I think it's good to mix and match. You can have the best of both worlds if you are careful - the girl can see her friends and you can see yours. My mates rubbed it in a bit when the relationship ended. I'd phone them up and ask if they wanted to go out. And they'd say they hadn't heard from me for so long they weren't sure if I was still their mate. I would never do that again. It's very important to keep in touch with your friends. Even now when I'm away the odd phone call, once a month or something, just to say hello, makes a big difference. I am into shy cute girls myself, not the ones who throw themselves over me. But they have to be independent girls too with minds of their own. I'm an Aquarius. I once read that Aquarius blokes like girls who stand up for themselves and hold back a little. They can't stand girls who become obsessive and who say they love you all the time. That's me. I like to be romantic if I get the chance with a girl. I once sent this girl a rose every hour all day on her birthday to this day she doesn't know who sent them. I like to take girls out to dinner and make them feel dead special and grown-up. I don't get much chance for that at the moment though.

People say I am quite mature for my age but I don't think I am that different to most kids of my age. It's just that I have had to grow up quickly in the last year and I think I have come on in leaps and bounds because of it.

I am the one everyone fancies so they tell me. I don't know why. I think I'm very flattered, but then again I don't like to say that I'm proud of it. At school I was like the quiet one. I always stood at the back. I remember once a girl came up and kissed me and I ran off crying. I think they thought I was the shy and cute one. I think it's just because I smile a lot.

Being called 'cute' is the worst thing about being a pop star along with your personal life and relationships having to take second best. I think a couple of the lads had serious relationships before we took off. I've never really got into anything major.It's really difficult to get anything steady going - it's not fair on the other half.

We see a lot of pretty people every day and obviously under different circumstances you might have fallen for each other. But there's no chance of that when we are working. You never get a chance to really meet many people, most of the time it's in and out. I'd like to get to know everybody that comes to see us a lot better than we can. In the early days the girls would come up and meet you and say things to you like I really want to get to know you. But nowadays as far as contact that way goes, it's very difficult. It's hard to talk to them when we're on the road. You go to places, meet girls and before you know it you're off again.

I do want a relationship eventually but I don't want to get tied down at the moment.I want to devote mtself to my fans. Without them there wouldn't be a Take That. When I'm going out I prefer to go out with my friends and catch up on all the latest gossip rather than chase girls. But when I go home and friends say they're going out with girlfriends, it seems as though it would be nice.

FAME, FORTUNE AND THE FUTURE

The boys, clearing up after the *Smash Hits!*
awards ceremony

GARY

❝ I'm very proud of the way we conduct ourselves. We always pay for our extras in hotels for instance, like drinks in the mini-bar and phone-calls. Not many bands do that but we control the money very carefully, and that sort of thing teaches us to keep a value of things. I don't know how much money is really coming in now but we are all sort of living a poor man's life at the moment.

In some respects being famous is as good as I thought it would be. But in others it isn't. The worst aspects are that you just seem to lose the plot of life - the simple things like going home and cooking, for example. Fortunately I now have my own home so I can go back and relax on my own. I've turned into a bit of a mini housewife. I say, 'Ooh, there's a nice furniture shop', and all the lads laugh at me. I've more or less achieved all the ambitions I had now and maybe it's time to sit down and make a whole new list of them because that's what I do

On tour in the USA: Lady Liberty attracts 5 new fans

every year. I miss things like going down to the supermarket for eggs if I've forgotten to get some. Now if I go, there will be a load of people wanting autographs. You do think how much longer can I take this? There's as many good parts as there are bad parts. The highlight is when press people come and you get good write ups - that's the big buzz. Even though we're pop stars now, when I meet other stars I still expect them to be something magical, and it's never like that. George Michael is my idol, but I don't really want to ever meet him because I think I'd probably be disappointed. I prefer to know him as I do as a great singer and great songwriter.

The one group we most look up to is probably the Beatles when they were at their height. They were young blokes having a laugh just like us but they handled themselves well and didn't take themselves too seriously.

With an eye to the future, Gary realises that should he ever leave Take That, there's a new career for him as a yellow cab driver. . .

. . . while Jason prefers the police force

JASON

❝ I never thought it could be like this. I just never dreamed that it would come this far. When we first got together it was like, yeah this is good fun. As a schoolboy I always thought something was going to happen because I've always danced and I've always looked to be a bit of a showman on stage. And I thought that if I carried on then someone's going to see me eventually and I might end up being someone dead smart. But it was still a massive surprise. I don't think I deserve it; there is so much talent out there that doesn't get recognised. I was just in the right place at the right time - and I've worked hard. I am very ambitious. I'd like to speak several languages, and learn to play seven instruments - small things like that. My biggest wish is just to be really happy. I'm happy enough as it goes, but I'd like to be buzzing all the time. Maybe a family will bring me that, maybe old age will, I don't know. Maybe it means making a million and giving it all to charity.

I would describe myself as changeable. Sometimes I look at myself and wonder what kind of person I am. It's like one minute I could feel like this and then the next day I could feel like that. I've become very ambitious, determined, passionate in things I'm doing. I'm doing new things every day like learning Spanish and the guitar. I enjoy going to different countries,

Mark, of course, plans to always remain a superstar!

Poised to take Manhattan by storm

Robbie, Jason and Gary calling home

meeting new people, getting to know people, getting to know their culture.

We don't have much money at the moment but when we do I'd like to buy somewhere nice for my mum. I just love to support my family, the only thing wealth means to me is security.

I love the adoration but it doesn't go to our heads. It's a job, like when I was decorating. Getting away on a Friday was as satisfying as playing a good gig! The girls are very tempting, obviously, but we are never alone with them long enough for anything to happen. We do the gig and five minutes later we are back in the hotel.

I never dreamed we'd be where we are now - it's incredible. We got together for fun, now it could be a million pound business. It's great. I get a bit tired but it's a small price to pay isn't it?

I feel like I've changed, I feel I'm changing every day. I think I've matured and I'm growing up very fast. We've got all this responsibility on our shoulders and we had to get wise to the superficial people and the whole superficiality of the business. I know where I'm going. I'm part of the lads and they are part of me and we're all part of this project, it gives us a direction.

Goodbye, America!

It's quite an impressive s - t - r - e - t - c - h limo!

HOWARD

"I think a lot of people like to imagine fame has changed me. But the truth is that a lot of people's attitudes towards me have changed. I think they assume that you are pretentious and big headed, but me personally I don't think I've changed in the way I act: I'm still as down to earth as I ever was and I don't ever want to change. I haven't had many people say it to my face, but I can tell it in the approach. They might think that I'm different, but if they speak to me then they will soon know that I'm the same Howard Donald.

Japan was my favourite place. I imagined it to be more traditional with temples, but it's more skyscrapers and lots of buildings, very expensive and very busy. We went on the bullet train to Osaka which was amazing. Definitely my best experience yet."

Times Square - and time to be going home

ROBBIE

" We all do get on well, they're like my best friends. There is not one that I couldn't tell any of my problems to and I mean the deepest problems. I suppose that's good because a lot of bands have friction between themselves, and I couldn't cope with that sort of tension.

We have a strict manager and he keeps us in order. Two years ago he warned us of everything that was going to happen. He said, 'You're going to have to tell your mums and dads you've got to go ex-directory, you're going to have girls waiting outside your house and you are going to have to be careful.' We didn't believe him then but all these things have happened now, one by one. We're not superb angels. But we are careful and we know the score.

When we first started out we were hiring a minibus to get to gigs. Now we're flown everywhere and driven in a limousine; we're being spoilt and all, but I don't think it will ever change us. Sometimes we'd rather travel in our van. We still have a good laugh which is what's kept us going.

Hello, Japan : Mark makes a new friend

In the bullet train to Osaka

I still have a lot of mates from old but there's a gap between us now obviously. When I'm away I don't get time to turn around, let alone phone anyone. When I go out with my mates it takes an hour before they fall back in and I fall back in to being their mate again. In your mind it can be really big time, but if you step back and look at it, it's all a game.

We're given a wage every month. Money is something that I've never experienced before and I went mad with it at first. I was out there buying flash clothes, everything was on me. Now I'm thinking money, it's got to be kept - so that's what I'm doing with it. If we go over the top and start buying things, Nigel will come up and say things like, watch yourself. And I go, oh yeah, because he's right. He always is when it comes to money. When I've asked him for next month's wages now please, because I've spent it, he tells us no and we go with whatever he says.

The most interesting places for me have been Canada and Japan. We got mobbed everywhere we went and that revitalised us because we were all a bit knackered. It's really easy to get very tired and it's going to get harder over the next few months, but I think we can all cope with it. We've been through a lot from the beginning until now and we've coped with everything they've thrown at us so far. The itinerary is like Belgium, a day in Sweden, a day in Germany, back to Spain for three days, back to Germany for two days - it's all bits and bits and bits. But that's OK, its a job and I wouldn't be doing anything else.

But Mark, the language of love is universal!

Chocoholic Gary eating sushi - or are they Belgian pralines, Gary ?

Making even more friends: hopefully Robbie's realised the two women to his left are dummies!

The boys enjoying a stroll around Tokyo before the hectic tour schedule starts

The fans are are great. There is nothing that gives you more of an adrenalin buzz than being somewhere with 2,000 girls outside waiting for you to come out of the television studio. Or selling out a concert tour in two hours. But at the same time I want to get home more often. I only get home every once in a while for two or three days at a time. And when I'm at home I want to be with my parents and everything. But there's a knock at the door every two minutes with fans wanting to come in or I'm changing my telephone number. I can't believe how many people have got my address. One letter got to me with Robbie Williams, Port Vale, Stoke-on-Trent on the envelope. It's a strange feeling because its everything I've ever dreamed of: I've always wanted to be famous. There's a line in the George Michael song 'Freedom' - *I was every young school girls pride and joy* and I guess that's how it is for us now.

I am nineteen and work is coming first. I want to be happy with my finances by the time I am twenty-four/twenty-five and not to have to worry too much about things. That's my ultimate goal. I have a few friends that have stayed by me. But the band are my best friends. A lot of people don't know how to talk to me anymore because they've seen me on the telly. I personally think I haven't changed. I hope I haven't changed, but peoples attitudes towards me have changed. I'd describe myself as a very confused paranoid schizophrenic and they're the better points.

The boys looking a little cramped in the back of a Japanese van

In Japan, every fan has a camera

Mark with two geisha girls - obviously the book he was reading earlier paid off!

Goodbye, Japan!

Which way to the gents?

MARK

“ Winning seven awards at the Smash Hits show was amazing. We were delighted with all our awards especially those which were chosen by the public. They mean more to us than, say, the Brit Awards that are chosen by the industry. There has been a lot said about us and the New Kids. They have got where we will hopefully eventually get to, but one day somebody is going to come along and take our place; we realise that.

It’s been fantastic to travel the world. My favourite place was New York, though I really enjoyed Japan as well. I’d like to carry on having success but at the end of the day we’ve had a great laugh and so long as I end up happy, then that’s the most important thing. ”

Take That must be superstars if they get to appear with Mr Blobby!

DiSCOGRaPHY

DATE	TITLE	CHART POSITION
	SINGLES	
July 1991	DO WHAT U LIKE	82
November 1991	PROMISES	38
January 1992	ONCE YOU'VE TASTED LOVE	47
May 1992	IT ONLY TAKES A MINUTE	7
August 1992	I FOUND HEAVEN	15
September 1992	A MILLION LOVE SONGS	7
December 1992	COULD IT BE MAGIC	3
February 1993	WHY CAN'T I WAKE UP WITH YOU	2
	ALBUMS	
August 1992	TAKE THAT AND PARTY	2
	VIDEO	
December 1992	TAKE THAT AND PARTY	1

Fans wishing to join the *Take That Fan Club* should write for an application form to:

New Members Department
· Take That Fan Club
P.O. Box 538
MANCHESTER
M60 2DX